The World of Whimble Whimsy

Fanciful Fabric Projects for the Heart & Home

Welcome All and Follow if you please The Footsteps To the Quiet World of the Whimbles

Annabelle's Gate at
"The Enchanted Place"

The World of Whimble Whimsy

Fanciful Fabric Projects for the Heart & Home

MARTHA YOUNG

STERLING PUBLISHING CO., INC. NEW YORK
A STERLING/CHAPELLE BOOK

Chapelle Ltd.

Owner: Jo Packham

Editor: Linda Orton

Staff: Areta Bingham, Kass Burchett, Jill Dahlberg, Marilyn Goff, Holly Hollingsworth, Susan Jorgensen, Barbara Milburn, Karmen Quinney, Cindy Stoeckl, Kim Taylor, Sara Toliver, Desirée Wybrow

Photography: Kevin Dilley, for Hazen

Library of Congress Cataloging-in-Publication

Young, Martha, 1943-
    The world of Whimble whimsy : fanciful fabric projects for the heart and home / Martha Young
        p. cm.
    Includes index.
    ISBN 0-8069-4449-8
    1. Textile crafts. 1. Title.

TT699 .Y68 2001   2001040083
746--dc21

10 9 8 7 6 5 4 3 2 1

A Sterling/Chapelle Book

Published by Sterling Publishing Company, Inc.
387 Park Avenue South, New York, NY 10016
© 2001 by Martha Young
Distributed in Canada by Sterling Publishing
c/o Canadian Manda Group, One Atlantic Avenue, Suite 105
Toronto, Ontario, Canada M6K 3E7
Distributed in Great Britain and Europe by Cassell PLC
Wellington House, 125 Strand, London WC2R 0BB, England
Distributed in Australia by Capricorn Link (Australia) Pty Ltd.
P.O. Box 704, Windsor, NSW 2756, Australia

Printed in China
All Rights Reserved

Sterling ISBN 0-8069-4449-8

Every effort has been made to ensure that all of the information in this book is accurate.

If you have any questions or comments, please contact:

Chapelle Ltd., Inc.
P.O. Box 9252
Ogden, UT 84409

Phone: (801) 621-2777
FAX: (801) 621-2788
e-mail: chapelle@chapelleltd.com
website: www.chapelleltd.com

Whimble Designs, Inc.

WHIMBLE DESIGNS is a collaboration between Martha Young and Jock McQuilkin. The couple grew up together in upstate New York. One wintry evening after dancing school, Jock hurled a snowball at Martha. Somehow they were able to transcend this experience to become best friends. After dating for several years, their lives separated. Jock pursued a career in investments, eventually cofounding his own money management firm in Boston. Years later, Fate intervened. The childhood sweethearts reunited, were married in 1994, and shortly thereafter launched Whimble Designs. The business encompasses Martha's three-dimensional work as well as her two-dimensional stationery products, and home accessories. Whimble Designs is housed in a renovated commercial building in midtown Atlanta.

Owners: Jock McQuilkin and Martha Young

Illustrator: Martha Young
Designer: Martha Young
Design Workshop: Angela Evans, Angela Garrett,
Sara Landbeck, Julia Lintern
Production Manager: Katy Munroe
Retail Manager: Kelly Schneider
Retail Assistant: Michelle Aftousmis

Acknowledgments:
Designer: Lisa Block
Graphic Design: Isa Williams Design, Inc.
Photographer: Kelli Coggins
Architectural Renderings: Kemp Mooney, Architect
Former Design Assistants: Rachelle Capes, Carrie Murtha
Building and Project Manager: Mickey Patrick
Accounting Managers: Tracy Walker, Mary Miller

Dedication:
I would like to dedicate this book to the enduring support
of my husband and professional partner, Jock McQuilkin.

Message from the Anciennan, Thallo:
"In case you were wondering, Companions and Friends refer
to Lumenist Whimbles as 'Master' and 'Mistress.'"

Whimble Designs, Inc.
1540/42 Monroe Drive, NE
Atlanta, Georgia 30324

404.892.0492   fax 404.892.3733
toll-free 877.944.6253

www.thewhimbles.com

To Nadine—
With best wishes
from The Whimbles
Martha Young
02·16·06

About the Author

MARTHA YOUNG and her husband, Jock McQuilkin, are the cofounders of Whimble Designs, Inc.,
in Atlanta, Georgia. Having received both a BA and an MVA, Martha has concentrated not only in art history but is
also trained as an illustrator and is an experienced art educator. Years ago, she began creating three-dimensional figures
embellished with antique snippets of lace, buttons, and other interesting materials. She describes her artistic process
as an "immersion in an elegant world of enchantment where one fantasy continually connects with the next, resulting
in a glimpse of an ethereal and whimsical world." Whimble Designs is a combination studio workshop and retail store
into which Martha's characters and stories are woven. Known also as "The Enchanted Place," it is Martha's vision
made manifest where her beloved Whimbles work and play every day to help others realize their dreams.

Table of Contents

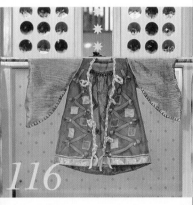

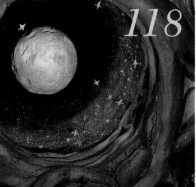

Thaddeus' Orb

Caelumen

Eternal Spring

The Story of The Whimbles

WITHIN A SMALL, ANCIENT LAND CALLED ZIR lies an even smaller hidden one known as Caelumen. This miniature land is watched over by King Thaddeus who reigns from a great orb centered directly above Caelumen and its two kingdoms, Ancienna and Lumenesia.

Ancienna is composed of several territories. It has always been the home of the wise Anciennans, ageless creatures who for long periods of time reside within Caelumen's deep core until King Thaddeus summons one to ascend from this underworld upward through the pure waters of the Eternal Spring. This being finally bursts forth from the center of the magical Blue Lotus Flower just as the Sun, Revelato, spreads its rays over the surface of the mirror shiny spring water. When the sacred blue petals gracefully open to the Sun and the Anciennan steps over them to the water's edge, he knows, as all others who have taken this journey before him, that he will be dream master, storyteller, teacher, and guide to all who know him.

The other kingdom, Lumenesia, is linked by colonies, named for their denizens—tiny creative beings called Whimbles. These creatures enjoy the simple pleasures of life: a cozy home, tea and tasty food celebrations with friends and companions, storytelling, indoor and outdoor gardens, and most especially, the art of sewing. When certain Whimbles develop extraor-

King Thaddeus watches over Caelumen from his orb.

dinary sewing and tailoring skills, they are touched by King Thaddeus' Golden Butterfly on Caelumen's longest day of the year celebration, "The Day of Pure Dreams." From that day forth, they are known as Lumenists, an honor which bears two great responsibilities. The first is that they create magical garments called "Coats of Light" which will protect and manifest the dream of any being who wears one. The second is to respect their unerring ability to recognize whose dreams are pure and whose are not, for it would be very dangerous indeed for a coat to be created and worn by someone whose dreams are not authentic and truly heartfelt.

A grassy mesa on Caelumen called The Spine vertically separates the land into its two neighboring kingdoms much like the halves of a fruit. It is the major arterial pathway leading north and south, providing the lifeline between the two kingdoms. One dark winter night long, long ago, this pathway was destroyed. The sacred stones at The Spine's very pinnacle were toppled, and an earthquake resulted, shaking the land. Tremors lasted for days. When they ended, Caelumen lay divided, her spine broken. The catastrophe only signified the beginning of Caelumen's destruction. Over time conditions worsened. The light which had shimmered throughout the land dimmed in Lumenesia. As the kingdom lay dying, King Thaddeus sent an Anciennan on an arduous journey to the uppermost reaches of Lumenesia. Through this Anciennan's courage, sacrifice, and faith in the face of great doubt and fear, The Spine was restored and the land was healed.

When the sacred blue petals gracefully open to the Sun and the Anciennan steps over them to the water's edge, he knows,… that he will be dream master, storyteller, teacher, and guide to all who know him.

In recent years, King Thaddeus has sensed a similar dimming of light on the planet Earth. He has worried endlessly wondering how he might help. As always, he let his dreams guide him. One dawn, he had a vision of a woman who could interpret Caelumen's world to other humans. He called her Elysia although she is known on Earth as Martha. As he dreamed his dream for her world, he knew she was dreaming of his miniature one so far away. When the king's Golden Butterfly announced himself to her, she knew it was time for their shared vision to be realized.

King Thaddeus called his messenger butterflies to The Palace of Light in Chrysalis. When the last alighted on his throne, he spoke to them. "Go to Caelumen. Tell everyone about a world far, far away where the skies are darkening much as ours did so very long ago." The butterflies' antennae quivered and their lovely wings began to open and close nervously.

The king continued, "Beings there called humans are confused. They have forgotten many of their fine, pure ways and their traditions have been tarnished. I have chosen Lumenists from each colony to journey to this land called Earth. A special welcoming

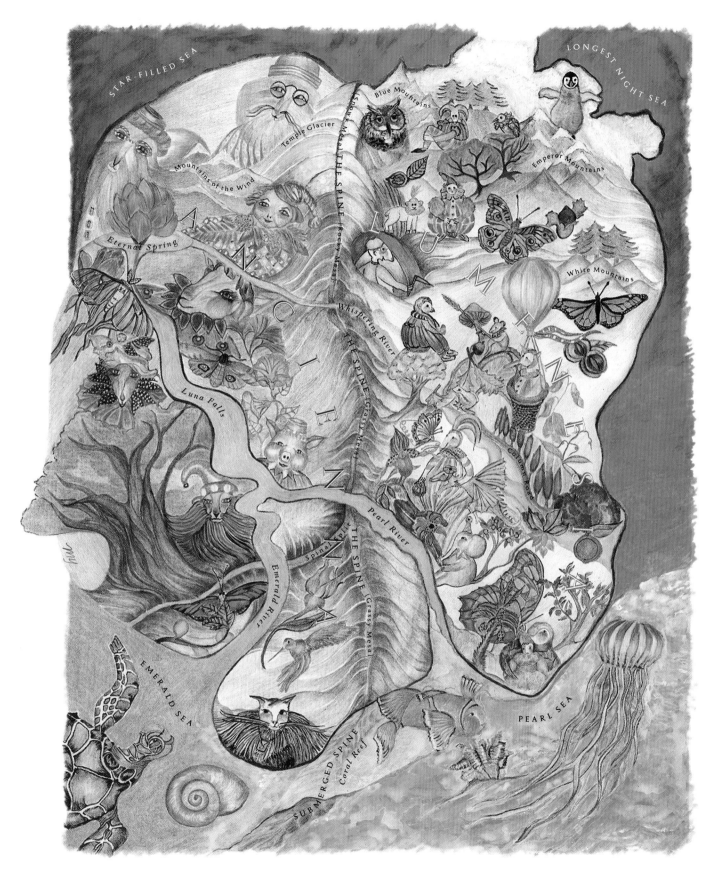

STAR-FILLED SEA

LONGEST NIGHT SEA

Temple Glacier

Blue Mountains

Mountains of the Wind

Snow Mesa THE SPINE (Rocky Mesa)

Emperor Mountains

Eternal Spring

A N C I E N T

White Mountains

Whispering River

THE SPINE (Grassy Mesa)

Luna Falls

E N Z A

Caravan Road

Pearl River

Spinal Spur

THE SPINE (Grassy Mesa)

Emerald River

EMERALD SEA

PEARL SEA

SUBMERGED SPINE Coral Reef

home filled with light called 'The Enchanted Place' has been prepared for them there. It has underground tunnels, winding roots, bubbling waterfalls, and thriving plant life much like Caelumen. Once the Lumenists arrive, they will guide those in 'The Enchanted Place' to create good work from fabric and ribbon, to spin elegance from snippets and scraps. They will create 'Coats of Light' which will enable humans to rediscover that pure dreams may indeed come true. I know many will be attracted to the magic in this place."

The butterflies heard their king's words. Soon they departed and spread the news to all of Caelumen. On a sunny breezy day that spring, several Anciennans strode down a pathway from the West toward a Lumenesian group on a knoll below them. The excited colorful gathering consisted of Lumenists from each of the six colonies, their beautiful birth butterflies, and their special companions and friends. Bulging wicker luggage, leather bound Books of Patterns, and sewing baskets with collections of thimbles and needles, fabrics, ribbons, beads, and buttons rested in the tall grass.

Anciennan Cat, Thallo

Suddenly, two figures ran hurriedly from beneath an ancient beech tree. Brothers Wendell and Jacob, Hillside Lumenists, were late as usual. Out of breath, they bowed before the Anciennan Cat, Thallo.

"Master Thallo, we just finished the wee necklace pouches you requested. We hope you like them," they said as their ears bobbed up and down.

Thallo took the pouches from Wendell. He felt them for some time. "They are perfectly made, Wendell and Jacob, exactly what I wanted."

The cat called each Whimble forward. After putting a pouch over each of their heads, he placed two gifts into their outstretched hands. "It is time to give you two presents from your Anciennan friends. One is our snippet journal in which you will find many of our Anciennan sayings. May it always remind you of the power of our friendship. The other is a silver container filled with magic bubble potion. You only have enough to blow two large strong bubbles to surround you and your fellow voyagers: one to reach your destination and one to return to your beloved Caelumen. May they protect you during your travels." As each Whimble received his gifts, he placed them in his pouch for safekeeping.

Within moments, six perfectly round iridescent bubbles lifted gently from the grassy knoll and soon disappeared from sight. For many weeks the bubbles floated through unfamiliar

Silver container filled with just enough magic bubble potion
to protect the Whimbles on their journeys to and from "The Enchanted Place."

skies until late one night the silence was pierced by a shrill cry. "There it is," Brill, the Hillside Whimble House Wren, announced.

"I see it now, too! It's the shiny thimble atop a copper roof! Brill, you have the finest eyesight!" replied Jacob excitedly.

"This is King Thaddeus' exact description!" chimed Thalia, Jacob's birth butterfly.

Wendell and Jacob guided the other five bubbles down slowly, ever closer and closer to the silver thimble resting above "The Enchanted Place." Moments later, they landed—their journey from Caelumen safely over; but they knew as they climbed from their bubbles, that their adventures in their new home had just begun.

Many will be attracted to

the magic in this place.

CHAPTER ONE

Early Morning in
The Hidden Courtyard Garden

"Good morning and welcome to everyone! I'm Wendell."

"And I'm Wendell's twin brother, Jacob. We're Hillside Whimbles. We've been waiting for you among the pansies just beyond Annabelle's Gate. You can see that we are so small that we could fit in the palm of your hands. We could even hide in one of your coat pockets."

"This is our home away from home, isn't it, Jacob?"

"Oh! Yes, it is, Wendell! So much has been carefully built around us to remind us of Caelumen although as you can see, I often carry a staff with the image of our moon, Vesperata, on it. I could never forget her."

"We do miss our colonies in Lumenesia and the wise Anciennans, but we are also enjoying the many new friends we have met since we arrived here."

"You humans know this place as the fairy-tale store called Whimble Designs, but we call it 'The Enchanted Place.'"

"Since Jacob and I led the other Lumenesians from Caelumen, they thought we should be your guides here."

"Since we are all tiny, we would be ever so appreciative if you would be really careful not to step on any of us while we lead you about."

"Also, Wendell and I need to ask you to talk softly. Some of us are quite shy and are frightened of loud noises."

Hillside Lumenists, Wendell and Jacob, guide visitors through "The Enchanted Place."

"Manning, the Woodland Whimble, is guardian of our hidden courtyard garden here. He is motioning to us. We just need to walk up the rock steps along the forest stream to reach him. Do you see the necklace pouch he is wearing around his neck? Both Jacob and I made them for all the Whimbles who made this voyage. I can see that Manning is carrying an egg in his. You can fashion either a small one like his or a larger one for your special treasures."

Ribbon Necklace Pouch

Instructions from Hillside Whimble Lumenist, Wendell

Materials needed:
10" x 5" piece of muslin
10" x 5" piece of silk lining fabric
3½ yards of ⅝"-wide silk ribbon
5 yards of ½"-wide silk ribbon
Silver thread
Various beads
Fray Check™

1. Cut one of each pattern from muslin fabric.
2. Cut one of each pattern from lining fabric.
3. Beginning at one long edge of one muslin piece, sew the ⅝"-wide ribbon down along edge of the muslin piece.
4. Overlap a second piece of ribbon over the first piece ⅛" and stitch ribbon edges down.
5. Continue until muslin piece is covered in ribbon.
6. Do the same for the other piece of muslin.
7. Place the two ribboned pieces with right sides together and stitch along the sides, leaving the top open.
8. Turn right side out.
9. Stitch lining pieces with right sides together along the sides, leaving a 1" opening along one side for turning later. Leave top of lining open.
10. Cut 20 varied lengths (1½"–3") of the ½"-wide ribbon for fringe.

11. Line up the fringe pieces along the top of the ribboned pouch and stitch in place.
12. Sew lining and ribbon pouch with right sides together at top, turning right side out through 1" opening in lining.
13. Close the opening in the lining by hand.
14. Press lining to the inside of pouch.
15. Cut two 4½"-long strips of the ⅝"-wide ribbon.
16. Turn under ends ¼".
17. Sew to outside top edge of each side of the ribbon pouch for a casing for the drawstring.
18. Chain crochet the silver thread into two 7"-long pieces for the drawstring.
19. Thread through the openings of the ribbon casing and knot on each side.
20. Chain crochet the remaining ½"-wide silk ribbon into a 36"-long strap, leaving 2"–3" of uncrocheted ribbon on each end.
21. Sew the strap on each side by hand just above the drawstring opening, leaving the ribbon piece dangling.
22. Thread 3–4 beads on ribbon piece at each end of the strap and knot at the bottom.
23. Thread 2–4 beads on the end of each piece of the fringe, knot at the end.
24. Fray Check the ends of all the fringe pieces.

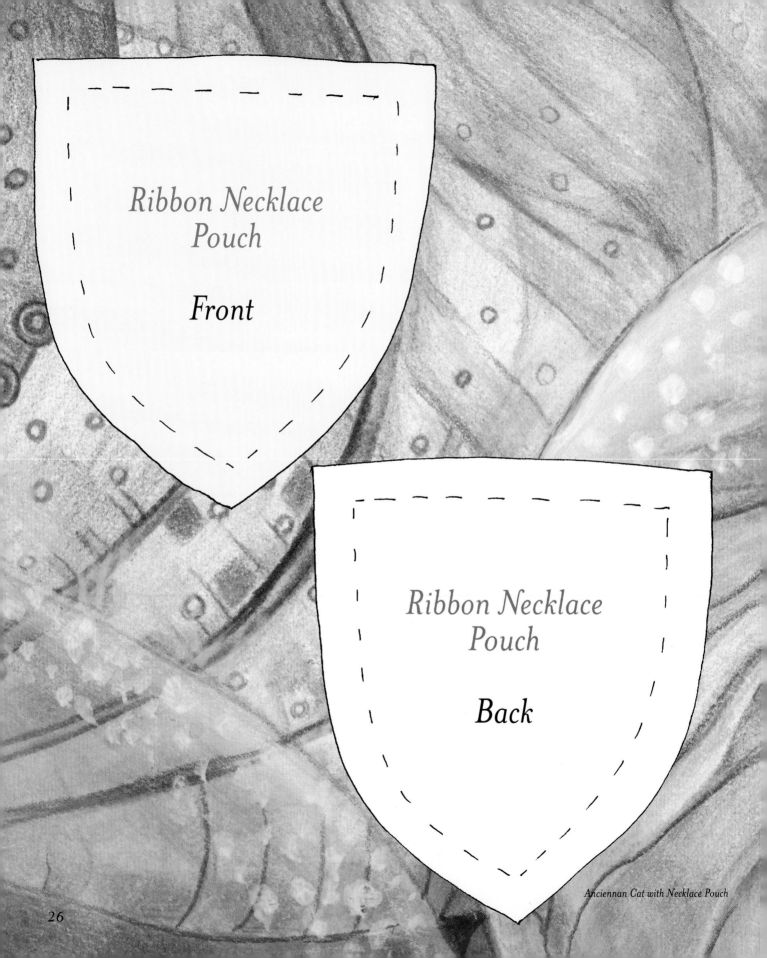

Ribbon Necklace
Pouch

Front

Ribbon Necklace
Pouch

Back

Anciennan Cat with Necklace Pouch

Envelope Pouch

Instructions from Hillside Whimble Lumenist, Jacob

Materials needed:

12" x 6" piece of tapestry fabric
12" x 6" piece of silk brocade for lining
1 yard of ½"-wide organza ribbon
4 yards of ½"-wide silk ribbon
4" beaded trim
Fray Check™

1. Cut one of each pattern (front and back) from tapestry fabric.

2. Cut one of each pattern piece from silk fabric.

3. Sew all but three strands of beads onto bottom of right side of front tapestry piece.

4. Sew remaining three strands of beads onto center front side of the pouch flap.

5. Place the two tapestry pieces with right sides together and sew up to the first mark.

6. Place the two silk pieces with right sides together and sew up to the first mark, leaving a 1" opening along one side for turning.

7. Sew the tapestry and the silk lining with right sides together along the flap and the front edge, leaving an opening between marks on pattern for the drawstring.

8. Turn right side out through 1" opening in lining.

9. Close opening in silk lining by hand.

10. Press lining to the inside of pouch.

11. Stitch a line ⅜" from the top of the front edge and across the two marks as indicated on "envelope pouch back" pattern.

12. Cut the ½"-wide organza ribbon in half.

13. Thread organza ribbon through openings left for drawstring in pouch.

14. Knot organza ribbon at ends and Fray Check.

15. Cut ½"-wide silk ribbon into three equal pieces.

16. Braid silk ribbon together and knot at ends.

17. Sew the strap on each side by hand just above the drawstring opening.

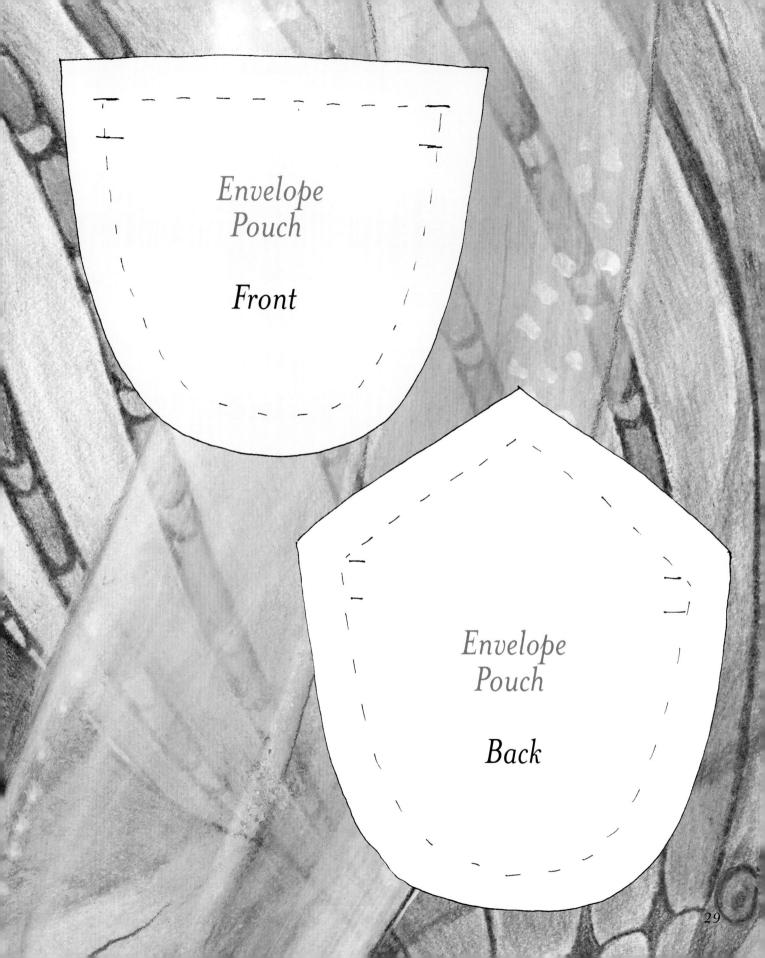

Envelope
Pouch

Front

Envelope
Pouch

Back

Wee Whimble Pocket Pouch

Instructions from Hillside Whimble Lumenist, Wendell

Materials needed:

3" x 5" piece of muslin
3" x 5" piece of silk lining fabric
2 yards of ½"-wide silk ribbon
Silver thread
Various beads
Teenie Tassel
Fray Check™

1. Cut two of pattern in muslin fabric.
2. Cut two of pattern in lining fabric.
3. Beginning at one long edge of one muslin piece, sew the ½"-wide ribbon down along edge of the muslin piece.
4. Overlap the next piece of ribbon ⅛" over the first piece and stitch ribbon edges down.
5. Continue until muslin piece is covered in ribbon.
6. Do the same for the other piece of muslin.
7. Place the two ribboned pieces with right sides together and stitch along the sides, leaving the top open.
8. Turn right side out.
9. Stitch lining pieces with right sides together along the sides, leaving a 1" opening along one side for turning later. Leave top of lining open.
10. Cut 20 varied lengths (½"–1½") of the ½"-wide ribbon for fringe.
11. Line up the fringe pieces along the top of the ribboned pouch and stitch in place.
12. Sew lining and ribbon pouch with right sides together at top, turning right side out through 1" opening in lining.
13. Close the opening in the lining by hand.
14. Press lining to the inside of pouch.
15. Cut two 2"-long strips of the ½"-wide ribbon.
16. Turn under ends ¼".
17. Sew to outside top edge of each side of the ribbon pouch for a casing for the drawstring.
18. Chain crochet the silver thread into two 5"-long pieces for the drawstring.
19. Thread through the openings of the ribbon casing and knot on each side.
20. Chain crochet the remaining ½"-wide silk ribbon into a 12"-long strap, leaving 1"–1½" of uncrocheted ribbon on each end.
21. Sew the strap on each side by hand, just above the drawstring opening, leaving the ribbon piece dangling.
22. Thread 3–4 beads on ribbon piece on each end of the strap and knot at the bottom.
23. Thread 2–4 beads on the end of each piece of the fringe, knot at the end.
24. Fray Check the ends of all the fringe pieces.
25. Sew tassel to bottom of pocket pouch.

Wee Whimble
Pocket Pouch

"Now he's pointing up toward the elm tree. I wonder if Annabelle . . ."

"Jacob and Wendell, would you just look at her? How many times have I told her not to go up in her Thimballoon when the breeze is strong. She could get tangled again in a tree or worse! Oh! There's Gillian, that poor Field Mouse is climbing furiously along the tree branch to reach her and bring her back safely. I can't imagine how many times he has rescued her."

"Manning, you know that Gillian has been her companion since he was born. He knows her ways so well that he's always one step ahead of her. He'll keep her safe from harm."

"I know, Jacob, but that Sweet Pea Whimble is just so stubborn. When she wants to sail in her Thimballoon, there is no stopping her! Then something happens when she's in the air. She forgets to think. She just daydreams. Before long she's in the next colony."

"I'm guiding her down now,

     Master Manning.

        No need to worry!

           Just enjoy our guests."

Even the handrails have butterflies and flowers decorating them to remind us of our Caelumen home.

"Oh my! I do apologize for not wishing all of you the top of the morning before now. You see I always love to greet any being who enters this garden. It is so much like the woods of my Lumenesian colony with its small maple trees and waterfalls. Even the handrails have butterflies and flowers decorating them to remind us of our Caelumen home."

"Manning, our visitors love your spring pennant collar almost as much as your pouch. They've never seen one before. Could you tell us about it?"

"I think Sophie had just a few scraps left after we finished our nest. 'The Enchanted Place' workshop was very generous with their materials. We have made a most elaborate home."

"Manning, I think Sophie would be more than happy to tell everyone how to make not only a pennant collar, but also one of her gay snippet collars as well. We all admire the ones she made for Martha's animal who she calls a dog. His name is Pippin. We all used to be frightened of him because he was very loud, but now he is much quieter. We speak to him almost every day, and he has told us that some cats here on Earth can wear these collars too."

Snippet Collars

Instructions from Woodland Whimble Lumenist, Sophie

Materials needed:
14" piece of ¼"-wide cording
46" piece of 2"-wide sturdy ribbon
75 snippet strips of ½"-wide fabric or ribbon
   in various textures and colors

1. Place cording in center of 2"-wide ribbon.
2. Fold ribbon in half over cording.
3. Stitch in place.
4. Tie snippets with knots over cording,
   leaving 16" at each end for tying.
5. After tying snippets, trim them evenly.

Pippin in his Snippet Collar

Small Pennant Collars *(This is a Whimble serger project)*

Instructions from Woodland Whimble Lumenist, Sophie

Materials needed:

25" piece of ³/₄"–1"-wide sturdy ribbon
Snippets of various 4"-square fabrics
Machine embroidery thread

1. Cut ten triangles from the various fabrics.
2. Serge around edges with machine embroidery thread.
3. Leave serger tail at point of triangles.
4. Fold flat tops of triangles over ¹/₂".
5. Stitch ³/₈" from edge, leaving casing opening.
6. Thread the 25" piece of sturdy ribbon through triangles.
7. Gather triangles together to 9" at center of ribbon, leaving 8" of ribbon on each side for tying.

Small Pennant Collar

Medium Pennant Collars *(This is a Whimble serger project)*

Instructions from Woodland Whimble Lumenist, Sophie

Materials needed:

28" piece of ³/₄"–1"-wide sturdy ribbon
Snippets of various 4¹/₂"-square fabrics
Machine embroidery thread

1. Cut ten triangles from the various fabrics.
2. Serge around edges with machine embroidery thread.
3. Leave serger tail at point of triangles.
4. Fold tops of triangles over ¹/₂".
5. Stitch ³/₈" from edge, leaving casing opening.
6. Thread the 28" piece of sturdy ribbon through triangles.
7. Gather triangles together to 12" at center of ribbon, leaving 8" of ribbon on each side for tying.

Pippin in his Medium Pennant Collar

Large Pennant Collars *(This is a Whimble serger project)*

Instructions from Woodland Whimble Lumenist, Sophie

Materials needed:

31" piece of ¾"–1"-wide sturdy ribbon
Snippets of various 5½"-square fabrics
Machine embroidery thread

1. Cut ten triangles from the various fabric squares.
2. Serge around edges with machine embroidery thread.
3. Leave serger tail at point of triangles.
4. Fold tops of triangles over ½".
5. Stitch ⅜" from edge, leaving casing opening.
6. Thread the 31" piece of sturdy ribbon through triangles.
7. Gather triangles together to 15" at center of ribbon, leaving 8" of ribbon on each side for tying.

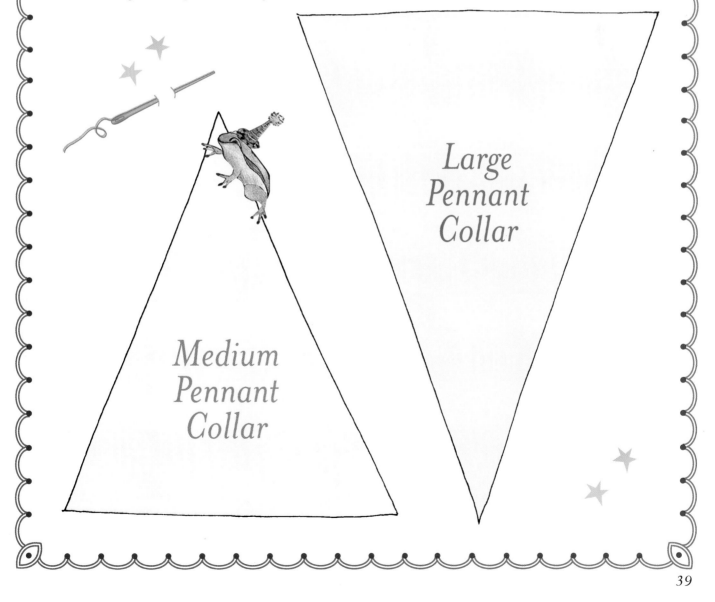

Large
Pennant
Collar

Medium
Pennant
Collar

"Manning, I also want to teach everyone how to make a nest as colorful as ours. They can even add beads and buttons and any other found objects just like we do. And we can't forget to show them how to fill their nest with a beautiful egg."

Small Nest *(This is a Whimble serger project)*

Instructions from Woodland Whimble Lumenists, Sophie and Manning

Materials needed:

$6\frac{3}{4}$ yards of $\frac{1}{8}$"-wide cable cording
$6\frac{3}{4}$ yards of 20-gauge copper wire
12" x 6" pieces of 5 different pastel silk fabrics
(or $1\frac{1}{2}$"-wide silk ribbon in 5 different colors)
Machine embroidery threads

1. Cut fabric into $1\frac{1}{2}$" x 12" lengths, resulting in four strips of each color.
2. Cut 20 pieces of cording into 12" lengths.
3. Cut 20 pieces of wire into 12" lengths.
4. Lay one piece of cording and wire onto center of each fabric strip.
5. Fold in half lengthwise and stitch against the cording.
6. Thread serger with decorative embroidery threads.
7. Run edges of fabric/cording pieces through serger, leaving thread tails of 3"–4".
8. Coil strips into a nest shape, beginning with the base and working toward the top edge.
9. Intertwine the strips together.
10. Hand-stitch in place as needed.

Medium Nest *(This is a Whimble serger project)*

Instructions from Woodland Whimble Lumenists, Sophie and Manning

Materials needed:

$6\frac{1}{4}$ yards of $\frac{1}{4}$"-wide cable cording
$6\frac{1}{4}$ yards of 20-gauge copper wire
15" x 5" pieces of 5 different pastel silk fabrics
(or $1\frac{1}{2}$"-wide silk ribbon in 5 different colors)
Machine embroidery threads

1. Cut fabric into $1\frac{1}{2}$" x 15" lengths, resulting in three strips of each color.
2. Cut 15 pieces of cording into 15" lengths.
3. Cut 15 pieces of wire into 15" lengths.
4. Follow Steps 4–10 of Small Nest, above.

Large Nest *(This is a Whimble serger project)*

Instructions from Woodland Whimble Lumenists, Sophie and Manning

Materials needed:

$8\frac{1}{2}$ yards of $\frac{1}{4}$"-wide cable cording
$8\frac{1}{2}$ yards of 20-gauge copper wire
15" x 6" pieces of 5 different pastel silk fabrics
(or $1\frac{1}{2}$"-wide silk ribbon in 5 different colors)
Machine embroidery threads

1. Cut fabric into $1\frac{1}{2}$" x 15" lengths, resulting in four strips of each color.
2. Cut 20 pieces of cording into 15" lengths.
3. Cut 20 pieces of wire into 15" lengths.
4. Follow Steps 4–10 of Small Nest, above.

Whimble Project Packet Available

Small, Medium, and Large Egg Pillows

Instructions from Woodland Whimble Lumenist, Manning

Materials needed:

9" x 24" piece of silk
9" x 24" piece of muslin
1 yard each of 2 different ½"-wide
    silk ribbons
1 yard of ½"-wide organza ribbon
1 large bead
4 seed beads
ClusterFil®
Monofilament thread

1. Cut 6 of pattern in silk.
2. Cut 6 of pattern in muslin.
3. Place each silk piece on top of a muslin piece.
4. Stitch each set together ⅛" from edges.
5. Keep silk sides together and match top mark.
6. Stitch pieces together at sides with ¼" seam
    allowance. The top of egg will be closed when
    stitching is finished.
7. Turn right side out and stuff with ClusterFil.
8. Close the bottom of egg with a hand-gathered stitch.
9. Stitch ¼" from bottom edge and work seam allowance
    to inside of egg.
10. Wrap organza ribbon around one seam of the egg.
     Tie in a bow at top.
11. Do the same with the other two silk ribbons,
     covering all the seams of the egg.
12. Sew one seed bead at the base of the egg.
13. Sew the large bead in center of bows at top of the egg.
14. Secure the large bead in place with remaining three
     seed beads.

Whimble Project Packet Available

Small Egg

(Cut 6)

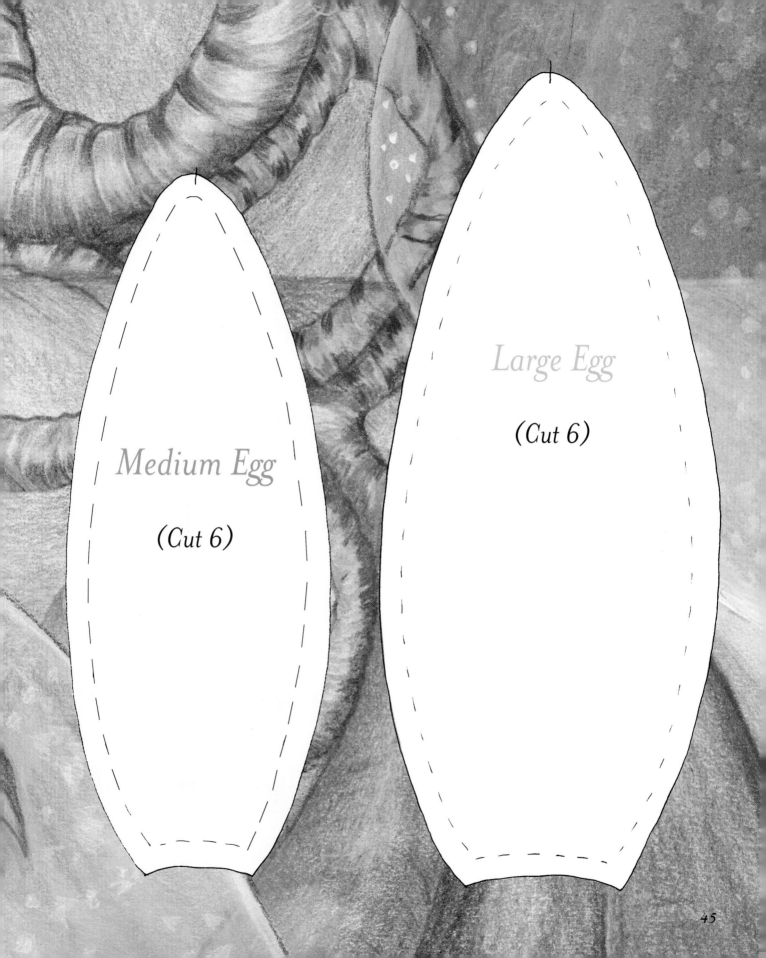

Medium Egg

(Cut 6)

Large Egg

(Cut 6)

*A ceramic Majolica Stafford,
the Tiny Tree Frog, wearing
one of his favorite party hats.*

"Stafford, I see you on that maple leaf. Come out and say hello to everyone. They love your party hat, especially the little girls and boys. We all have party hats in Caelumen. Dougal, the Elephant Sprite, a close friend of Thomas, the Water Whimble, wears party hats as much as you do, Stafford. Thomas makes hats for him all the time and told us that he would share his pattern when we talk to him."

"You know I'm shy, Master Wendell; and being a green tree frog, I can blend in with leaves anytime I want. But since I love all my bright party hats, I know you can find me as easily as Rufus and Margaret when we play hide and seek."

"As you know, Wendell, Sophie and I could not have done without our companion, Stafford. Our children were born so soon after we arrived here at "The Enchanted Place" that we were overwhelmed. He has protected them each day while we care for this garden."

"Mistress Sophie, I see them now. They're right above us in the elm tree near their small birdhouse. What a racket they make with all that chirping!"

"They're just trying to tell our visitors about the patterns of them you created, Stafford. They are so perfect that both Master Manning and I would be pleased if you would share them."

"It's a bit embarrassing for me but if you insist, I will fetch them right away."

Woodland Whimble Children, Margaret and Rufus
Instructions begin on page 48.

Margaret
Woodland Whimble, Manning and Sophie's Daughter

Instructions from Stafford, the Tiny Tree Frog, Manning's Companion

Materials needed:

5"-square piece of pink velvet
7" piece of ½"-wide white eyelet lace
12" piece of ½"-wide pink silk ribbon
Flat crystal bead
Round pink bead
Small white feather
Paper clay
Gouache watercolors in white, peach, brown, and black
Clear spray sealer
Craft pellets
Craft glue

1. Cut one of body pattern from velvet.
2. Using a gathering stitch, hand-gather ⅛" from edge of circle.
3. Fill with pellets.
4. Pull gathering stitch tight and knot, leaving a ¼" opening for the head.
5. Gather eyelet lace into circle and set aside.
6. Gather pink silk into circle and set aside.
7. Shape paper clay into a ½" sphere, pulling a portion of the clay down into a "neck" shape.
8. Add a small oval on each side for "cheeks."
9. Shape paper clay into an "upper beak."
10. Shape paper clay into a "lower beak."
11. Attach beaks to sphere between cheeks.
12. Let clay dry thoroughly.
13. Mix equal parts of peach and white paint.

14. Base-coat head.
15. Use peach paint for cheeks.
16. Use brown paint for beak.
17. Use black and white paints for eyes.
18. When paint is dry, spray with clear sealer.
19. Place lace and silk ribbon as collars on top of body.
20. Put neck through collars into body, gluing into place.
21. Glue clear crystal bead on top of head.
22. Glue pink bead on top of crystal bead.
23. Glue feather into pink bead.

Margaret
Body

Rufus

Woodland Whimble, Manning and Sophie's Son

Instructions from Stafford, the Tiny Tree Frog, Manning's Companion

Materials needed:

5"-square piece of blue velvet
7" piece of 1/2"-wide striped ribbon
Flat crystal bead
Round blue bead
Small white feather
Paper clay
Gouache watercolors in white, peach,
   brown, and black
Clear spray sealer
Craft pellets
Craft glue

1. Cut one of body pattern from velvet.
2. Using a gathering stitch, hand-gather
   1/8" from edge of circle.
3. Fill with pellets.
4. Pull gathering stitch tight and
   knot, leaving a 1/4" opening for
   the head.
5. Gather striped ribbon into circle
   and set aside.
6. Shape paper clay into a 1/2" sphere,
   pulling a portion of the clay down
   into a "neck" shape.
7. Add a small oval on each side
   for "cheeks."
8. Shape paper clay into an
   "upper beak."
9. Shape paper clay into a "lower beak."
10. Attach beaks to sphere between
    cheeks.
11. Let clay dry thoroughly.
12. Mix peach and white paint together.
13. Base-coat head.
14. Use peach paint for cheeks.
15. Use brown paint for beak.

16. Use black and white paints for eyes.
17. When paint is dry, spray with clear sealer.
18. Place ribbon as collar on top of body.
19. Put neck through collar into body,
    gluing into place.
20. Glue clear crystal bead on top of head.
21. Glue blue bead on top of crystal bead.
22. Glue feather into blue bead.

Rufus
Body

"Oh! Jacob. Now look who's coming around the bend downstream!"

"Why here come, our new feathered friends, Kirsty and Lorna, they are out and about on this fine spring morning."

"Yes, we certainly are. I'm teaching Lorna how to swim downstream. Oh! Watch out, Lorna! You're too young a duckling to be paddling that fast! You'll go right over the waterfall again and irritate the goldfish, Claudette, in her pond."

"That's better. Now let's just practice swimming around the Whimbles' maple tree island for awhile before going inside at noon for a short roost."

"Kirsty, before you do go, would you tell us more about the velvet duck and duckling patterns that the workshop here has completed? I know you have guided them in the creation of these designs."

"I would be honored. I can tell you I am particularly proud of little Lorna's pattern."

Lorna, the Duckling

Kirsty, the Duck and Lorna, the Duckling
Instructions begin on the page 52.

Kirsty, the Duck ★

Instructions from Kirsty, the Duck, Friend of the Whimbles

Materials needed:

25" x 18" piece of white or yellow velvet (for body)
18"-square piece of orange velvet (for beak and feet)
16" x 22" piece of decorative fabric (for clothing)
1½ yards of 1"-wide ribbon
3 yards of variegated ½"-wide ribbon
2 large beads
Craft pellets
ClusterFil®
Small white feathers
Eyes
Craft glue
Yellow embroidery thread

1. Cut two of body pattern from velvet.
2. Cut four of wing pattern from velvet.
3. Cut two of tail pattern from velvet.
4. Cut two of beak pattern from orange velvet.
5. Cut four of feet pattern from orange velvet.
6. Sew body with right sides together, leaving a 1" opening in the back for turning and stuffing.
7. Sew two wing pieces with right sides together, leaving a 1" opening for turning and stuffing.
8. Repeat with remaining two wing pieces.
9. Sew tail with right sides together, leaving a 1" opening at the top for turning and stuffing.
10. Sew two feet pieces with right sides together, leaving a 1" opening for turning and stuffing.
11. Repeat with remaining two feet pieces.
12. Sew beak with right sides together, leaving a 1" opening at the top for turning and stuffing.
13. Turn all pieces right side out.
14. Stuff the wings, feet, tail, and beak with ClusterFil only.
15. Stuff the body with ClusterFil, stuffing tightly through the neck area.
16. Add pellets in the bottom ¼ of duck body.

17. Close the openings in the wings, feet, tail, and body with small hidden stitches.
18. Stitch wings to body by hand.
19. Stitch feet to body by hand.
20. Stitch tail to body by hand.
21. Fold seam allowance inside ¼" at top of beak.
22. Pin beak in place on duck's face.
23. Embroider duck's beak in place with yellow embroidery thread.
24. Using french knots, make nostrils at top of beak.
25. Make a small slit on each side of head for eyes.
26. Insert eyes and glue in place.
27. Glue small white feathers around the eyes.
28. Glue feathers on top of head.
29. For the clothing, cut two of coat front pattern from decorative fabric.
30. Cut one of coat back pattern on fold.
31. With right sides together, sew front and back coat pieces at side seams and shoulder seams.
32. Make a ¼" rolled hem along edges and neckline.
33. Coil 1"-wide ribbon into circular hat shape.
34. Stitch into place.
35. Cut ½"-wide variegated ribbon into four equal pieces.
36. Sew two ribbon pieces onto hat for ties.
37. Sew remaining two ribbon pieces onto coat at neckline for ties.
38. Thread beads onto end of ribbon on coat and knot ends.
39. Dress Kirsty, the Duck.

Kirsty, the Duck

Tail (Cut 2)

Kirsty, the Duck

Body (Cut 2)

*Enlarge All Kirsty, the Duck
Pattern Pieces 144%*

Kirsty, the Duck
Feet (Cut 4)

Kirsty, the Duck
Bill (Cut 2)

*Enlarge All Kirsty, the Duck
Pattern Pieces 144%*

Kirsty, the Duck
Wings (Cut 4)

Kirsty,
the Duck

Coat Front (Cut 2)

*Enlarge All Kirsty, the Duck
Pattern Pieces 144%*

Fold

Kirsty, the Duck

Coat Back (Cut 1 on fold)

Lorna,
the Duckling
Wings (Cut 4)

Lorna,
the Duckling
Bill
(Cut 2)

Lorna, the Duckling
Body (Cut 2)

Lorna, the
Duckling
Feet (Cut 4)

Lorna, the Duckling

Instructions from Kirsty's duckling, Lorna

Materials needed:

16" x 10" piece of blue velvet (for body)
10" x 20" piece of blue velvet (for wings)
19" x 7" piece of orange velvet (for beak and feet)
3½"-square piece of silk brocade for hat
18" piece of 1"-wide striped ribbon
1 yard of decorative yarn
1 yard each of 3 different colors of 4mm-wide
  silk ribbon
Craft pellets
ClusterFil®
Small white feathers
1 large white feather
Eyes
Craft glue
Yellow embroidery thread
4 small beads

1. Cut two of body pattern from blue velvet.
2. Cut four of wing pattern from blue velvet.
3. Cut four of feet pattern from orange velvet.
4. Cut two of beak pattern from orange velvet.
5. Sew body with right sides together, leaving a 1" opening in the back for turning and stuffing.
6. Sew two wing pieces with right sides together, leaving a 1" opening for turning and stuffing.
7. Repeat with remaining two wing pieces.
8. Sew two feet pieces with right sides together, leaving a 1" opening for turning and stuffing.
9. Repeat with remaining two feet pieces.
10. Sew beak pieces with right sides together, leaving a 1" opening at the top for turning and stuffing.
11. Turn all pieces right side out.
12. Stuff the wings, feet, and beak with ClusterFil only.
13. Stuff the body with ClusterFil, stuffing tightly through the neck area.
14. Add pellets in the bottom ¼ of duck body.
15. Close the openings in the wings, feet, and body with small hidden stitches.
16. Stitch wings to body by hand.
17. Stitch feet to body by hand.

18. Fold ¼" seam allowance inside at top of beak.
19. Pin beak in place on duck's face.
20. Embroider duck's beak in place with yellow embroidery thread.
21. Using french knots, make nostrils at top of beak.
22. Make a small slit on each side of head for eyes.
23. Insert eyes and glue in place.
24. Glue small white feathers around the eyes.
25. Glue small white feathers on top of head.
26. Glue large feather down the middle of back.
27. Cut one of hat pattern from decorative fabric.
28. Gather-stitch fabric into circle.
29. Cut a 4" piece of striped ribbon.
30. Sew ribbon onto gathered hat.
31. Cut a 2" length of striped ribbon.
32. Fold 2" length of ribbon in half.
33. Stitch to back of hat.
34. For the snippet collar, cut each of the 4mm ribbon pieces and yarn into eight equal pieces.
35. Tie each ribbon and yarn piece around the remaining striped ribbon, leaving 2" at each end for ties.
36. Sew four beads down the front of the duck for buttons.

Lorna, the Duckling

Hat

CHAPTER TWO

Mid Morning in Thimble Hall

"The door's open, Masters Wendell and Jacob. I've been waiting for you quite awhile!"

"I know, Brill. You have been tidying up in preparation for our guests. We're coming in right now."

"This entrance, although much, much larger, is like our Hillside Whimble ones carved inside our doors within giant hazelnut trees. They are made to look like the inside of a thimble. We also create narrow winding tunnels that lead from our door deep within the tree's roots where we live."

"I'd like to lead everyone down the hallway where we keep all the Whimble Books of Patterns."

"Brill, could you give everyone a chance to glimpse where our underground spring begins first?"

"Sasha, I get as excited as any other House Wren to show off a bit, but I know how proud you are of your internal stream and all the plants lining it. They are just as green as those in Lumenesia's Orchid Whimble Colony."

"Brill, we do love it here. Both Rudi and I often climb up one of our ribbon ladders to sleep in a lady's slipper orchid that's blooming. We also store our hand-sewn hearts in them."

"Rudi and Sasha, we all have received the most specially crafted tiny hearts from you Orchid Whimbles. I think everyone would love to know how you make them."

Rudi and Sasha love to store their hand-sewn hearts in lady's slipper orchids.

Brill, the House Wren

The Internal Spring
at Thimble Hall in
"The Enchanted Place"

"Elspeth? I see you sleeping under that fern. You have helped us for years with our velvet and silk hearts. Would you explain how to make them?"

"I'm only a simple Elfin Dragon, Master Rudi. You Whimble twins are so creative. I'm almost as shy as Stafford. Maybe . . ."

"Elspeth, we are certain you will have very fine instructions. Please come out here and begin!"

"I will do my best, Mistress Sasha."

Heart Sachet Ornaments ✳

Instructions from Elspeth, the Elphin Dragon, Sasha and Rudi's Companion

Heart Sachet

Materials needed:
$\frac{1}{8}$ cup dried lavender
6" x 3" piece of velvet or silk fabric
2" of $\frac{1}{2}$"-wide ribbon
2 beads
3" thin gold cording
Fray Check™

1. Fold fabric in half so you have a 3"-square piece.
2. Lay pattern on fabric and trace onto one side.
3. Sew around the edges of the traced heart shape with right sides together, leaving a $\frac{1}{2}$" opening on one side.
4. Trim excess fabric from around heart shape leaving a $\frac{1}{8}$" seam allowance.
5. Turn heart right side out.
6. Stuff with lavender.
7. Close the opening with tiny invisible stitches.
8. Cut a point on each end of the ribbon and apply Fray Check to the ends.
9. Knot the gold cording together at one end and stitch to the top of the heart.
10. Lay the ribbon over the top of the heart and cording so it overlaps each side of the heart.
11. Sew the ribbon down on each side with the beads.

Please Do Not Disturb

"Belinda, our birth butterfly, is a very close friend to Elspeth. Years ago, she asked us if we would create a pattern of Elspeth. It took us quite a time to decide which fabrics, ribbons, and other embellishments to use, but we think we've figured it out now."

Elspeth,
the Dragon
Head (Cut 2)

Elspeth,
the Dragon
Wings (Cut 2)

Elspeth, the
Elphin Dragon
Body (Cut 2)

Elspeth,
the Dragon
Legs (Cut 4)

Elspeth, the
Dragon
Hat

Elspeth, the Elfin Dragon

Instructions from Orchid Whimble Lumenist Twins, Sasha and Rudi

Materials needed:

10"-square piece of white panne velvet

5" x 10" piece of white lace

3 yards of 7mm-wide silk ribbon

18" of 1"-wide white wired ribbon

25–30 seed beads in shades of white and pink

15 flat beads

5–10 small pearl beads

Two 13"-lengths of 20-gauge copper wire

1 yard of silk ribbon

6" piece of lace

ClusterFil®

Watercolor pencils

Body

1. Fold white velvet in half with right sides together.
2. Place pattern pieces on the velvet, pinning them securely.
3. Sew around the patterns carefully. Pay attention to the small curves, particularly those on the head.
4. Leave a ½" opening at the top of each leg.
5. Leave a ½" opening at the base of the neck.
6. Leave a ½" opening at the top of the body.
7. Remove pattern pieces and trim closely around stitching.
8. Turn each piece right side out.
9. Stuff with ClusterFil.
10. Sew across opening of the head.
11. Fit head snugly into the body opening.
12. Sew head securely in place.
13. Sew each leg opening closed by hand.
14. Pin legs to either side of the body so the figure sits upright on a flat surface.
15. Sew legs securely into place, concealing the stitch behind each leg.
16. Create the ridge on the back, using the 1"-wide white wired ribbon.
17. Fold wired ribbon in half lengthwise.
18. Using a gathering stitch, sew along length of ribbon at fold and gather the ribbon tightly.
19. Pin gathered ribbon into place from the base of the neck to the tip of the tail.
20. Sew securely into place.
21. You may wish to add beads to embellish the tail.
22. Embellish the front of the body with silk ribbons and small pearl beads.
23. Embellish the seam of the legs with the 7mm-wide silk ribbon.
24. Create ½" gathers, beginning at the base of each leg, and sew ribbon into place.
25. Add a seed bead every time you secure a stitch, repeat until you cover the seam extending to the toe.
26. Using a gathering stitch, sew along edge of 6" piece of silk ribbon for the collar.
27. Pull gathering stitch to join both ends to create a circle.
28. Stitch around neck of dragon, repeat with 6" piece of lace.

Wings

1. Cut 5" x 10" piece of lace into two 5"-square pieces.
2. Form wing shapes from wire, according to pattern.
3. Zigzag the wire ends together.
4. Place wing onto lace, zigzag around wire and trim.
5. Repeat with the second wing and remaining lace.
6. Wrap silk ribbon around and over stitched edges.
7. Sew wings into place on the dragon's back.

Hat

1. Cut one of hat pattern from snippet of lace.
2. Stitch along seam line, turn right side out.
3. Stuff with ClusterFil.
4. Sew onto top of dragon's head.
5. Embellish with ribbons and beads.

Face

1. Draw eyes and cheeks, using watercolor pencils.
2. Soften fabric when dry by rubbing gently over the marking with your fingers.

"Brill, both Rudi and I thank you for your patience. We will see you again this afternoon. Now you must lead our guests down the tunnel past all the lighted Books of Patterns that were brought from Caelumen."

"All humans need to know that these books have been, are, and always will be precious to all of us. The Whimbles constantly add to these patterns—new spring pantaloons for Annabelle, a vest for Manning, overalls for Rudi, a new collar for Sasha, new satin shoes for Thomas. It is endlessly exciting, isn't it, Wendell?"

"Yes it is, Brill. We refer to our patterns daily."

"While you fly down the hall guiding our visitors with Jacob, I will take the shortcut through the tree roots to our library. I have to gather some supplies to show everyone. Please meet me there."

"But of course, Master Wendell."

CHAPTER THREE

Noon in The Writing Room

"Hello there! Here I am down below the human-sized library table. Martha created miniature hallways, doors, and homes just for us in 'The Enchanted Place' so we can scoot from one area to another easily."

"Wendell and I use this door often since the writing room is one of our favorite places. We care for it just as Rudi and Sasha tend the internal spring garden. Often, Manning takes a rest from the hidden garden and joins us here for a cup of tea. Sometimes there is quite a gathering of us here and in the tree roots nearby. One day Brill began to add snippets and beads and buttons to one of Martha's illustrated cards that we keep in this area. It was such a good idea, that we often do them together. We have asked Brill if he would explain how we embellish our cards. It's such fun!"

Detail of Embellished Card

Wendell, the Hillside Lumenist, at a typical Whimble miniature door

Embellished Cards

Instructions from Brill, the House Wren, Wendell and Jacob's Companion

Materials needed:

Your favorite card
Glue
Your choice of the following:

- Assorted snippets of lace
- Assorted snippets of silk and organza ribbons
- Silk embroidery thread
- Ribbon
- Yarn
- Embroidery thread
- Beads
- Buttons
- Pearls
- Charms
- Old jewelry parts
- Tiny dried or silk flowers

1. Intertwine silk and organza ribbons with yarn and/or embroidery thread.
2. Tie various ribbons with more silk embroidery thread.
3. Lace a string of tiny beads through the length of the ribbon.
4. Glue interwined ribbons down the card.
5. Glue lace, flowers, and pearls to the card.
6. Add any other embellishments that you wish to make the creation your own.

As Brill says, "the more creative, the more beautiful!"

"I think the visitors to 'The Enchanted Place' love these cards, but I have noticed that many are just like me. They also have to wear glasses to see all the embellishments we have added."

"That's what gave us the idea to make them some beautiful ribbon eyeglass cases, isn't it, Jacob?"

"We liked the design so much that we created some for ourselves, too. Since you have made several for yourself, Jacob, would you please explain the instructions for both human- and Whimble-sized cases to everyone?"

"I would be honored, Wendell. Sometimes I have even added a cord to mine so I can wear it around my neck."

Ribboned Eyeglass Case

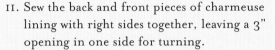

Instructions from Hillside Whimble Lumenist, Jacob

Materials needed:

2 yards of 1"-wide silk ribbon
6" x 12" piece of velvet
12" x 15" piece of silk charmeuse (for lining)
6" x 12" piece of muslin
1 tassel
1 decorative bead
100 seed beads

1. Cut one of front pattern from muslin.
2. Cut one of back pattern from velvet.
3. Cut one of front pattern from charmeuse.
4. Cut one of back pattern from charmeuse.
5. Take 1"-wide silk ribbon and place on top of muslin piece.
6. Hand-stitch ribbon in place with seed beads.
7. Continue, overlapping and bunching ribbon while stitching to muslin with seed beads.
8. Continue attaching ribbon and seed beads until entire muslin piece is covered.
9. Sew velvet back piece to ribbon front piece with right sides together.
10. Turn case right side out.
11. Sew the back and front pieces of charmeuse lining with right sides together, leaving a 3" opening in one side for turning.
12. With right sides together, sew the outside of the eyeglass case and the lining together at the top.
13. Turn right side out and close the opening in the lining.
14. Tack the lining and outside together at the bottom point to hold the lining in place.
15. Stitch along the fold in the flap to hold lining in place.
16. Finish with tassel at the bottom point of case.
17. Sew a decorative bead 1" down from the top of the front piece of the case.
18. Make a corresponding button hole at the tip of the flap.

Hillside Whimble Lumenist, Jacob

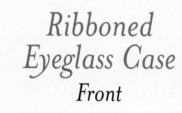

Ribboned
Eyeglass Case
Front

(Cut 2)
One in muslin to be ribboned
and one in charmeuse for lining

*Enlarge Ribboned
Eyeglass Case Pattern
Pieces 110%*

Enlarge Ribboned Eyeglass
Case Pattern Pieces 110%

Ribboned
Eyeglass Case
Back

(Cut 2)
One in velvet for backing and
one in charmeuse for lining

Wee Whimble Eyeglass Case

Instructions from Hillside Whimble Lumenist, Jacob

Materials needed:

2 yards of 1"-wide silk ribbon
4" x 12" piece of velvet
8" x 12" piece of silk charmeuse (for lining)
4" x 8" piece of muslin
1 tassel
1 decorative bead
100 seed beads

1. Cut one of front pattern from muslin.
2. Cut one of back pattern from velvet.
3. Cut one of front pattern from charmeuse.
4. Cut one of back pattern from charmeuse.
5. Take 1"-wide silk ribbon and place on top of muslin piece.
6. Hand-stitch ribbon in place with seed beads.
7. Continue, overlapping and bunching ribbon while stitching to muslin with seed beads.
8. Continue until entire muslin piece is covered with ribbon.
9. Sew velvet back piece and ribbon front piece with right sides together.

10. Turn case right side out.
11. Sew the back and front pieces of charmeuse lining with right sides together leaving a 1" opening in one side for turning.
12. With right sides together, sew the outside of the eyeglass case and the lining together at the top.
13. Turn right side out and close the opening in the lining.
14. Tack the lining and outside together at the bottom point to hold the lining in place.
15. Stitch along the fold in the flap to hold lining in place.
16. Finish with tassel at the bottom point of case.
17. Sew a decorative bead ½" down from the top of the front piece of the case.
18. Make a corresponding button hole at the tip of the flap.

Front

(Cut 2)
*One in muslin to be ribboned
and one in charmeuse for lining*

Back

(Cut 2)
*One in velvet for backing
and one in charmeuse for lining*

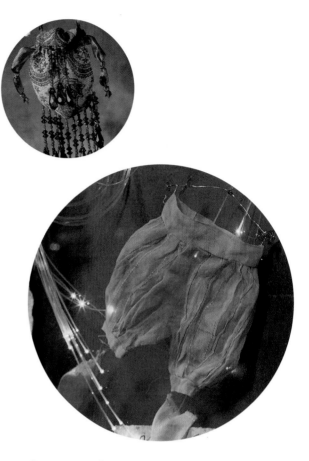

Jacob can always
be found in his
favorite spot deep
within the roots of
the ancient hazelnut tree
where he creates
wonderful gifts for
his dearest friends.

CHAPTER FOUR

Early Afternoon in
The Moon Dreams Nursery

"Masters Wendell and Jacob, I hear them whispering. They must be close by. Let me fly around the corner and see."

"Don't frighten them, Brill. They might just be waking from their early afternoon nap."

"I see all three. Devon, Dillon, and Delaney. Two of their companions, Ivy and Lilith, are with them, too."

"Oh, yes, Brill. They're waving from their balcony. From there, they can watch The Moon Dreams Nursery carefully. They do take such pride in their soft fluffy creations, which adorn this special room. Listen now! They're talking to us."

"We've been telling stories to the Fancy Lambs since our nap, Brill and Masters Wendell and Jacob."

"And Kyra, Ivy, and I always love Pillow Whimble tales."

"Where is Kyra, Lilith? She's not with you."

"She's not far. She has been with Sasha and Rudi, wading in the Internal Spring near the waterfalls. Her fur will be soaking again! Oh, I think I see them resting under the ferns. Yes! Look! Sasha's reading her a story now."

"Delaney, Sasha's using the bookmark that you made for her."

"Not only that, but she's sitting on one of your special tuffets, Dillon!"

"Ivy, the bookmarks for all of us were your inspiration."

"They were, and then you designed bookmarks for much larger human books, Delaney."

"I did. We each sew silky soft pillow puffs for our beds and sofas all the time. One day I decided to add one to each end of a ribbon and created a large bookmark. I think the humans like them because they like to read as much as we do."

"Delaney and Ivy, it would certainly please us if you would share these designs."

"That would be our pleasure, Master Wendell."

"Dillon, now it's your turn! Everyone of us here has one of your fine round tuffets. They are so soft and warm. Please share your creation with everyone."

Sasha and Rudi,
the Orchid Whimble twins,
plan a picnic with
Kyra, the Fancy Lamb.

Puff Bookmarks

Instructions from the Whimble Lumenist, Delaney, and his Companion, Ivy, the Fancy Lamb

Materials needed:

$\frac{1}{2}$ yard of $1\frac{1}{2}$"-wide silk ribbon
10" piece of $2\frac{1}{2}$"-wide silk ribbon
2 beads
2 seed beads
ClusterFil®

1. Cut the $1\frac{1}{2}$"-wide ribbon into one 12" length and four $1\frac{1}{2}$" lengths.
2. Cut the $2\frac{1}{2}$"-wide ribbon into two 5" lengths.
3. Take the $2\frac{1}{2}$"-wide lengths of ribbon, fold each in half and stitch ends together.
4. Gather-stitch $\frac{1}{8}$" in along the bottom of each piece.
5. Pull the stitching tightly and knot.
6. Stuff the two pieces with ClusterFil.
7. Gather-stitch $\frac{1}{8}$" in along the top of each piece.
8. Slip one end of the 12" piece of ribbon into the puff.
9. Pull the stitching tightly and knot.
10. Do the same with the other end of the 12" ribbon and the other puff.
11. Take four $1\frac{1}{2}$"-wide pieces of ribbon and fold into leaf shapes.
12. Stitch two ribbon/leaf pieces to the bottom of each puff.
13. Finish with a bead and seed bead on the leaves.

Pillow Whimbles, Dillon and Delaney, with their Companion, Ivy, the Fancy Lamb

Round Pillow Whimble Tuffet

Instructions from Pillow Whimble Lumenist, Dillon

Materials needed:

6" x 12" piece of white velvet
3"-square piece of velvet in a contrasting color
20" each of 8 different ribbons and/or yarns
Silver embroidery thread
I cup of dried lavender
2 covered buttons
ClusterFil®

1. Cut two of pattern from white velvet.
2. Sew around edges, with right sides together,
   leaving I" opening for turning and stuffing.
3. Turn velvet right side out.

4. Stuff velvet with combination of lavender
   and ClusterFil.
5. Close opening of tuffet with tiny hidden stitches.
6. Cover two buttons with contrasting velvet.
7. Sew one button in the middle of each side
   of the tuffet.
8. Braid yarns and ribbons together.
9. Stitch braid around the edge of the tuffet,
   using the silver embroidery thread.

Round Pillow Whimble Tuffet

(Cut two on fold)

"Kyra, we can all see that you are enjoying yourself with Sasha and Rudi, but could you come back here now? I need help with the instructions and pattern of the Fancy Lamb we drew together."

"Devon, I have had a perfectly idyllic afternoon, but I would never want to disappoint our guests. I'll be there in a Caelumen second."

Fancy Lambs

Instructions from Pillow Whimble Lumenist, Devon, and his Companion, Kyra, the Fancy Lamb

Materials needed:

4" x 8" piece of muslin
Mohair (doll's hair can be used as a
   replacement)
4 small twigs (approximately I½" long)
Gesso
Black and pink acrylic paints
8" piece of I"-wide silk ribbon
3" piece of 4mm-wide silk ribbon
I decorative bead
I seed bead
ClusterFil®
Hot-glue gun

1. Cut two of body pattern from muslin.
2. Sew around the body, leaving the marked area open.
3. Turn body right side out.
4. Fill body with ClusterFil.
5. Sew body opening closed with small, hidden stitches.
6. Mark holes for leg placement on bottom of body.
7. Slightly snip body at "x" marks.
8. Insert twigs into leg holes.
9. Check the height placement of the legs by standing the lamb upright before gluing in place.
10. Remove twigs.
11. Insert hot glue into leg holes.
12. Insert the twigs and allow to set in the glue.
13. Base-coat twigs completely with gesso for legs.
14. Base-coat the face area of the muslin with gesso.
15. Allow gesso to dry.

16. Apply a second coat of gesso on the legs only.
17. Allow gesso to dry.
18. Paint cheeks on face with the pink paint.
19. Paint eyes and nose on face with the black paint.
20. Cover body with mohair and hot-glue in place.
21. Pull apart mohair ringlets for added fullness.
22. Continue applying layers of mohair until desired thickness is achieved.
23. For collar, gather-stitch along one edge of I"-wide silk ribbon.
24. Pull stitching tightly.
25. Sew into place around the neck of the lamb.
26. Gather-stitch along one edge of 4mm-wide silk ribbon.
27. Gather ribbon into rosette.
28. Thread decorative bead and seed bead together and stitch onto rosette.
29. Hot-glue rosette and beads to lamb's head.

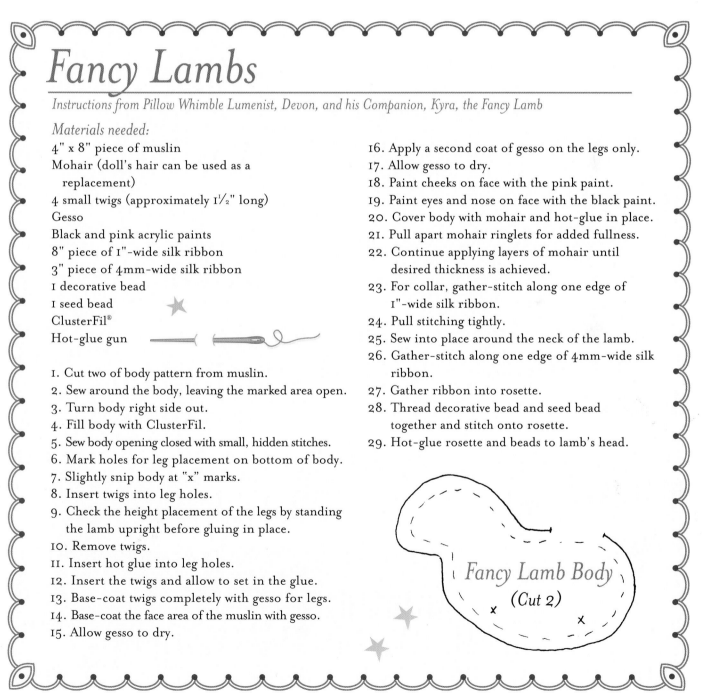

Fancy Lamb Body
(Cut 2)

CHAPTER FIVE

Mid Afternoon at Thomas' Waterfall

"Why, Thomas and Sebastian, what a fine afternoon for you to splash about in your waterfall! Have you also been swimming in Emmeline and Barnaby's pool just below you?"

"We certainly have, Wendell. Those two goldfish send you their best wishes. Just look at all the bubbles they are blowing to you!"

"I know you were pleased when you met them here at 'The Enchanted Place,' Thomas."

"Yes we were, Master Jacob. Even though our friend, the Elephant Sprite, Dougal, made the journey with us, both Thomas and I were very lonely here at first. We missed swimming in Caelumen's Pearl Sea with all our friends so much. Then, one day we met Emmeline and Barnaby. They are such special playmates, that we visit them everyday."

"We've told them about many of the animals and plants that live in our Pearl Sea. Sebastian particularly loves all the sea urchins living in our sea. For long periods of time he and I would observe them in the water. Emmeline told him that there are many living in the seas on Earth, too. So, my tiny sea turtle companion decided to create a pattern shaped just like a sea urchin. He then filled it with a most sweet smelling herb. Humans call this creation a lavender sachet."

"Sebastian, would you share this pattern with us?"

"I would be delighted, Masters Wendell and Jacob."

Sea Urchin Sachets

Instructions from Sebastian, the Tiny Sea Turtle, Thomas' Companion

Whimble Project Packet Available

Materials needed:

6" x 20" piece of charmeuse or china silk
Decorative machine embroidery thread
12" piece of 1"-wide silk ribbon
2½ cups of lavender

1. Serge top long edge of fabric.
1. Fold fabric in half with right sides together for a 6" x 10" piece.
3. Sew 6" ends of fabric with right sides together.
4. Gather-stitch ⅛" along unserged edge of fabric.
5. Pull gather-stitching to close the bottom end of fabric.
6. Secure the thread.
7. Turn sachet right side out.
8. Fill sachet with lavender.
9. Gather-stitch 1" in along top of sachet.
10. Pull top closed.
11. Secure thread.
12. Tie ribbon into a bow around the gathered top.

Sebastian, the Tiny Sea Turtle

Dougal, the Elephant Sprite,
in The Writing Room

"Hello there, everyone. I thought I would come say hello. I've just finished reading from the Snippet Journal in The Writing Room."

"Why Dougal, you surely travel fast. Jacob and I could never keep up with you!"

"You know all Elephant Sprites are very quick, Master Wendell. I'm no faster than any other in Lumenesia's Water Whimble Colony."

"Sebastian and I know Dougal is especially fond of our waterfall and all of the Internal Spring."

"Yes, Thomas, I am. Not only do I love to visit you both, but all the lush green plants and the water remind me of our home so far away."

"Thomas, I know you have finished the best pattern for an Elephant Sprite. Don't you think everyone here would love to see it?"

"Sebastian, how embarrassing, don't you think?"

"No, Thomas. Sebastian and I think it's a grand idea."

"Well, if you both really think so, then I'll agree; but then, Dougal, you have to tell our visitors about how to make the party hats that both you and Manning's Tiny Tree Frog, Stafford, love to wear."

"That's a fine idea, Master Thomas!"

Dougal, the Elephant Sprite

Instructions from Water Whimble Lumenist, Thomas

Materials needed:

12" of 3"-wide silk ribbon (for body)
5"-square piece of muslin
2 feathers
5" piece of cording
5" piece of 20-gauge wire
12" piece of 4mm-wide silk ribbon (for shoe accent)
4" piece of 1½"-wide silk ribbon (for legs)
4" piece of 1½"-wide silk ribbon (for shoes)
16" piece of ½"-wide silk ribbon (for leg cuffs)
12" piece of ½"-wide silk ribbon (for collar)
8 seed beads (for shoes)
12 seed beads (for collar)
4 seed beads (for head)
2 seed beads (for trunk)
2" piece of 4mm-wide silk ribbon (for trunk)
2" piece of 1½"-wide ribbon (for hat)
2 seed beads (for hat)
6" piece of 4mm-wide silk ribbon (for hat)
3 yards of 4mm-wide silk ribbon (for head decoration)
Gesso and paints
ClusterFil®
Craft Glue

1. Cut two of head pattern from muslin.
2. Stitch with right sides together.
3. Turn right side out.
4. Stuff with ClusterFil.
5. Cut four of ear pattern from muslin.
6. Stitch two ear pieces, with right sides together.
7. Turn right side out.
8. Stuff with ClusterFil.
9. Repeat with remaining two ear pieces.
10. Stitch ears to head between dots.
11. Base-coat head with gesso. Let dry.
12. Paint face with paints.
13. Sew ends of 3"-wide ribbon together.
14. Turn right side out.
15. With a gathering stitch, close the bottom.
16. Stuff with ClusterFil.
17. Gather-stitch along top of body.
18. Place head in opening.
19. Pull stitching tightly, holding head in place.
20. Cut ribbon for legs into 2" lengths.
21. Repeat with cording and wire.
22. Center one piece of cording and wire inside of ribbon.
23. With machine stitch, close the legs.
24. Cut ribbon for shoes into two equal pieces.
25. Fold ribbon in half lengthwise.
26. Stitch closed along both ends.
27. Turn right side out.
28. Sew to bottom of leg.
29. Sew top of shoe together, securing with thread and four seed beads.
30. Cut ribbon for shoe accent into two pieces.
31. Gather into a knot.
32. Stitch knot to toe of shoe.
33. Stitch legs to front of body.
34. Cut leg cuff ribbon into two equal pieces.
35. Gather and stitch body to top of legs.
36. Gather ribbon for collar.
37. Stitch onto elephant at neckline.
38. Decorate collar with seed beads.
39. Gather three yards of 4mm ribbon to decorate elephant's head.
40. Glue to the back of the elephant's head and around the face.
41. Glue two feathers to top of elephant's head.
42. Attach four seed beads to top of elephant's head.
43. Gather ribbon for trunk.
44. Glue to end of trunk.
45. Attach two beads for trunk decoration.
46. Coil ribbon for hat into a cone shape.
47. Gather hat decoration ribbon.
48. Sew at point of hat.
49. Attach two seed beads for decoration.
50. Stitch hat to top of elephant.

Dougal, the Elephant
Ear (Cut 4)

Dougal, the Elephant
Head (Cut 2)

Water Whimble Colony, Lumenesia

Wee Whimble Party Hats

Instructions from Dougal, the Elephant Sprite, Friend of Thomas, the Water Whimble

Materials needed:
5"-square piece of fabric
Fusible webbing
Bead
Seed bead
Bits of ribbon for trim

1. Cut two of party hat pattern from fabric.
2. Fuse together, following fusible webbing instructions.
3. Shape into hat, overlapping sides.
4. Sew in place.
5. Decorate with bead at the top and ribbon trim as desired.

Wee Whimble Party Hat

Dougal, the Elephant Sprite, created an extraspecial party hat for Thallo.

CHAPTER SIX

Late Afternoon at Annabelle the Baker's Cottage Tea Room

"Gillian is flagging us with his tail. Goodness, Wendell! It's already late afternoon, and we promised Annabelle that we would join her for tea. She has been baking shortbread heart cookies for everyone. I see her now, sporting her oven mitts and carrying a tray out of her moss cottage. I think it would be smart to hurry on over there!"

"You're right, Jacob. We better go quickly! Dougal, Thomas, and Sebastian, see you later at The Moon Window."

"I'm so pleased you brought our guests in time for tea, Wendell and Jacob. I had a little disaster with my first batch of shortbread heart cookies. I forgot to check the time. When I removed them from the oven, they were darker than I like."

"You mean they were burnt to a crisp, Mistress Annabelle!"

"Well, as I said they were too dark for my liking, so I'm relieved I had enough time to bake another perfect batch."

"Annabelle, both your jasmine tea and your cookies smell scrumptious. Wendell and I adore your sweets."

"Mistress Annabelle adores her own sweets, too. I have to watch that she doesn't eat too many of them."

"Why, Gillian, I have been limiting myself to two small cookies each day with my tea."

"Except for the ones you hide for late night snacks."

"Gillian, how could you think I would do such a thing?"

"We'll know for certain each time you climb into your Thimballoon. If you can't get off

Late afternoons are
always special at
"The Enchanted Place"
where cookies and
tea can be enjoyed.

Kenyon Rooney
2001

Do you suppose Annabelle has slipped a cookie
or two into her pocket?

the ground, or worse, cannot fit into it at all, we will know the truth, won't we Mistress Annabelle?"

"Gillian, my dear companion, you know that sweets are my weakness, but I am truly trying to be careful!"

"I do hope so, because it's springtime at 'The Enchanted Place,' your favorite time of year for taking to the air. I don't want to see you miss any Thimballoon rides, Mistress Annabelle."

"Um, Gillian, if we could interrupt your conversation, both Jacob and I had asked some time ago that you help Annabelle write down her delicious recipe for our guests."

"Yes, I remember, Master Wendell. I have it here for you."

"Jacob and Wendell, you know my spelling is not my strength. Gillian had to correct a few words."

"More than a few words, I have to say!"

"Let's just say we both worked hard on it, didn't we, Gillian? Then you wrote down your favorite icing recipe so everyone could decorate their cookies."

"I did, and we both hope everyone enjoys our confections."

Gillian the Field Mouse

Back side of Gillian

Annabelle's Shortbread Hearts

Instructions from Sweet Pea Whimble, Annabelle the Baker

Ingredients:
1 cup butter
½ cup sugar
1 tsp vanilla
2 ½ cups flour

1. Cream butter, sugar, and vanilla together until light and fluffy.
2. Stir in flour.
3. Chill several hours.
4. Roll dough ⅛" thick on lightly floured surface.
5. Cut with your favorite heart-shaped cookie cutter.
6. Transfer to cookie sheet.
7. Bake at 300°F for approximately 10 minutes (time will depend on cookie size) or until a light golden color.
8. Let cool slightly.
9. Remove from pan.
10. Decorate with icing.

Gillian's Favorite Icing

Instructions from Gillian, the Field Mouse, Annabelle's Companion

Ingredients:
4 oz. cream cheese
½ stick butter
1 pound of powdered sugar
1 tsp vanilla flavoring
1 tsp almond flavoring
3 tbsp. cream or milk
Food coloring

1. Beat all ingredients together until smooth.
2. Add food coloring.
3. Thin with cream as needed to achieve spreading consistency.

"Everyone loved Dougal's three party hats, Gillian. We know that you, too, love hats and that berets are your specialty. You have created them in various colors and fabrics for many Lumenesians here. I understand that you have made Annabelle so many that sometimes she can't decide which to wear when she's about to take to ride in her Thimballoon. It would please us greatly if you would share your pattern with our visitors. They will love it!"

"But of course, if you wish, Masters Wendell and Jacob."

"Master Wendell, since we have been discussing hats, I want to tell everyone about the golden crowns that you design for each and every one of us for our birthdays. Annabelle and I treasure ours, and we're certain every other Lumenesian here does, too. Would you be so kind as to share the secrets behind making these special crowns?"

"I would be delighted, Gillian. I love making them for all of you!"

Wee Whimble Berets

Instructions from Gillian, the Field Mouse, Annabelle's Companion

Materials needed:
3"-square piece of fabric
4" of $\frac{1}{2}$"-wide ribbon
Feather
Bead
Bits of ribbon

1. Cut one of hat pattern from fabric.
2. Sew ribbon together at ends, overlapping $\frac{1}{2}$" to form a $3\frac{1}{2}$" circle.
3. Gather-stitch around edge of fabric circle, pulling in stitching as needed to form a $3\frac{1}{2}$" dimension.
4. Stitch ribbon band to gathered fabric.
5. Decorate as you wish with feather, bead, and bits of ribbon.

Wee Whimble Birthday Crowns

Instructions from Gillian, the Field Mouse, Annabelle's Companion

Materials needed:
4" of gold braid trim
Craft glue
Tiny jewels or pearls

1. Glue braid into circle overlapping ends $\frac{1}{4}$".
2. Let dry.
3. Decorate with tiny jewels or pearls.

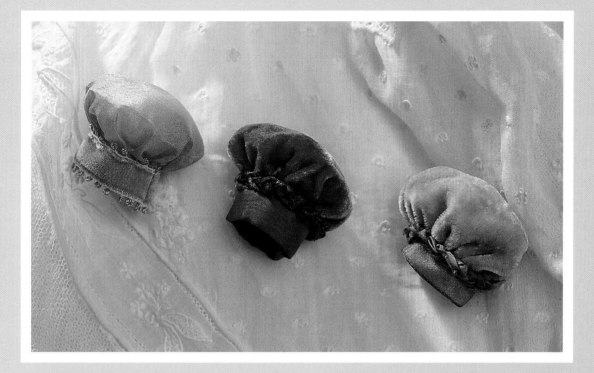

Above: Wee Whimble Berets
Left: Wee Whimble Birthday Crowns

Wee Whimble
Beret

CHAPTER SEVEN

Dusk in The Enchanted Workshop

"Masters Wendell and Jacob, can you hear the hum of the sewing machines?"

"Yes, Brill, we can, and undoubtably everyone else hears them, too. As we round this corner we will be entering 'The Enchanted Workshop.' There are special humans here who interpret our designs and patterns. You can see them sewing now."

"Because the workers here have wanted us to be in familiar surroundings, they have asked us how to create the decorations that adorn our Lumenesian homes. We described a few of these ideas and the workers created wonders. For example, Sophie created and collected many fine pieces of lace in Lumenesia. Although she keeps most safely tucked in a polished wooden linen chest, she has used a few to embellish her tree-house windows. She suggested that we cut an opening in our wall, place a lace sleeve between two pieces of glass, and *frame the glass and sleeve* to fit the opening."

Angela Garrett, Whimble designer

"Master Jacob, it is not only pretty to look at, but we can peek through this decorative opening from one room to the next."

"Brill, you're absolutely right. In addition, as Sophie has told us, now the lace is on view all the time and not hidden away in a drawer."

Julia Lintern, Whimble designer

A framed lace sleeve allows one to peek through.

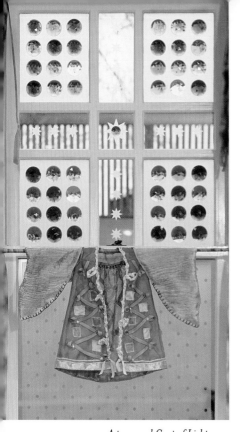

A treasured Coat of Light decorates a bejeweled window in "The Enchanted Workshop."

"Sasha's grandmother sewed some beautiful lace blouses for her to wear on special occasions. She talked with Martha and discovered that her grandmother also created blouses for her when she was a young girl. Sasha and Rudi suggested that Martha hang two of hers in her own workroom. From what you have told me, Wendell, Martha was delighted with the idea. She bought what humans call $\frac{1}{2}$"-diameter tension rods, wrapped them with a pale-peach silk ribbon, hung the starched *antique white lace blouses* on the rods, and opened the rods to fit the frame of her sandblasted windows."

"Master Jacob, I heard that Sasha rode around on Martha's shoulder giving her one instruction after the other. When the project was finished, Sasha was so happy she clapped her hands for minutes on end."

"She certainly did, Brill, because the blouses remind her so much of her own that she left behind in Lumenesia."

"After Sasha and Martha finished hanging her blouses, Jacob and I had our own idea for 'The Enchanted Workshop.' We cut and snipped and sewed a colorful *Coat of Light.* When we finished, we wrapped a tension rod with ribbon and hung our coat from it. Then we searched and searched for jewels like the ones we have in our home deep within the ancient hazelnut tree roots in The Blue Mountains of Lumenesia. When we found them, we applied them to the window above the coat. We hope that you enjoy what we've created."

"Masters Wendell and Jacob, both humans and Lumenesians love your beautiful handiwork."

Antique white lace blouses made by Martha's grandmother hang in her workroom,
thanks to a suggestion from Sasha, the Orchid Whimble Lumenist.

CHAPTER EIGHT

Nighttime at The Moon Window

"The birth butterflies are flying toward us—their flight signifying that the moon is rising, and that we must end our visit with one another at The Moon Window. All the other Lumenesians you have met will await us there."

"Master Wendell, I know we have but little time, but just before we gather together, could the butterflies give our visitors instructions for their Shadowbox Heart Sachets, a creation that is as delicate and beautiful as their wings?"

"Brill, you are the most insistent little bird, but we do love their sachets, too; and if they are speedy, they will have just enough time to share their project before we say farewell to our guests. Perhaps Manning's Paula could explain the instructions."

"I will gladly do so, Master Wendell, but I speak softly so everyone must listen very carefully."

118

Paula, Manning's birth butterfly

Shadowbox Heart Sachets

Instructions from all the Whimble birth butterflies

(W Whimble Project Packet Available)

(This is a Whimble serger project)

Materials needed:

4" x 8" piece of silk damask
6" x 12" piece of organza
2 large decorative beads
6 small round beads
12 seed beads
³/₄ cup lavender
Decorative machine embroidery thread

1. Cut two heart shapes from silk damask.
2. With right sides together, sew around edge, leaving a 1" opening.
3. Turn heart right side out.
4. Stuff heart thoroughly with lavender.
5. Close opening with small, hidden stitches.
6. At bottom of heart, sew 1 seed bead, 1 round bead, 1 decorative bead, and 1 additional seed bead.
7. Stitch a 3"-long piece of serger thread chain.
8. Sew serger chain to top of heart with 1 seed bead, 1 round bead, and 1 additional seed bead.
9. Cut organza into two 6" squares.

10. Attach top of serger chain to one corner of organza square.
11. Place second square of organza on top, enclosing the heart.
12. Pin organza pieces into place.
13. Serge around edges of organza, creating a 5½" finished square.
14. Finish bottom corner with serger thread chain.
15. Attach 1 seed bead, 1 round bead, 1 decorative bead, and 1 additional seed bead to bottom corner.
16. Finish remaining corners with 1 seed bead, 1 round bead, and 1 additional seed bead.
17. Braid a 4" serger thread chain.
18. Fold serger thread chain in half to create loop.
19. Secure loop at top corner of finished square.

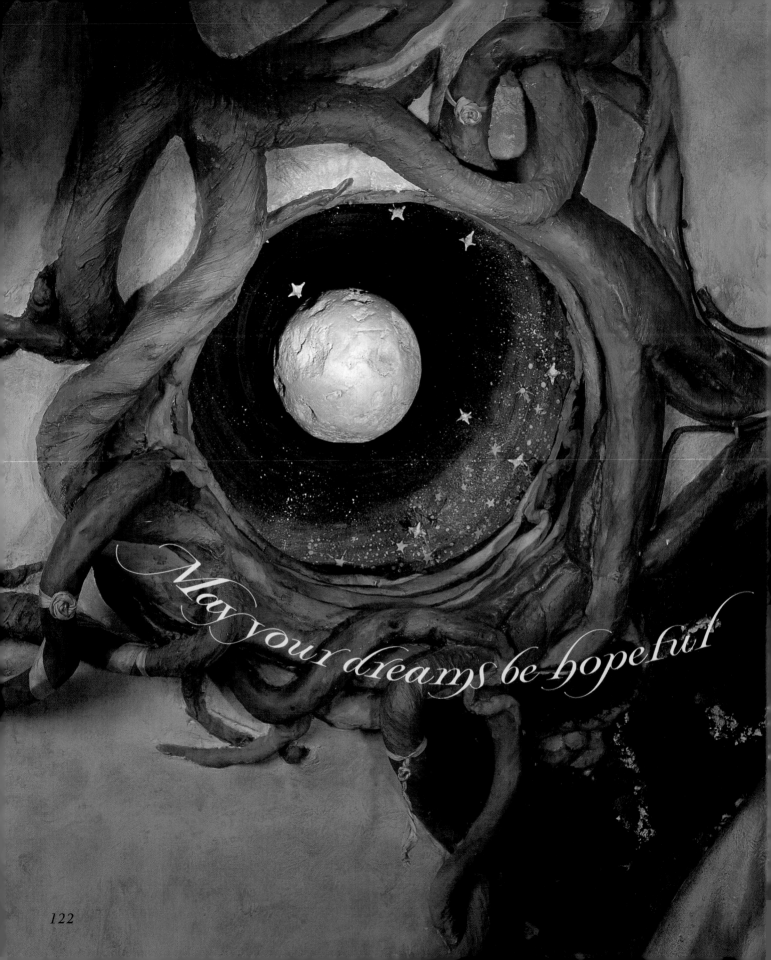

May your dreams be hopeful

"As we all gather together in The Moon Dreams Nursery, Wendell and I would like to tell you how pleased we are to have spent such a perfect day in 'The Enchanted Place' with you. As we bid you farewell, we ask you to pause for a moment with us at The Moon Window to honor your Earth's full moon and the stars in your heavens."

"We love your moon because she reminds us of our own, Caelumen's beloved Vesperata. Both cast a glow lighting the dark sky, our hearts, and our dreams. When you sleep tonight, may your dreams be hopeful. When you awaken, may your day be filled with brilliance."

and your days filled with brilliance.

Night of Wonder by Martha Young

Metric Conversion Charts

inches to millimetres and centimetres

inches	mm	cm	inches	cm	inches	cm
1/8	3	0.3	9	22.9	30	76.2
1/4	6	0.6	10	25.4	31	78.7
3/8	10	1.0	11	27.9	32	81.3
1/2	13	1.3	12	30.5	33	83.8
5/8	16	1.6	13	33.0	34	86.4
3/4	19	1.9	14	35.6	35	88.9
7/8	22	2.2	15	38.1	36	91.4
1	25	2.5	16	40.6	37	94.0
1 1/4	32	3.2	17	43.2	38	96.5
1 1/2	38	3.8	18	45.7	39	99.1
1 3/4	44	4.4	19	48.3	40	101.6
2	51	5.1	20	50.8	41	104.1
2 1/2	64	6.4	21	53.3	42	106.7
3	76	7.6	22	55.9	43	109.2
3 1/2	89	8.9	23	58.4	44	111.8
4	102	10.2	24	61.0	45	114.3
4 1/2	114	11.4	25	63.5	46	116.8
5	127	12.7	26	66.0	47	119.4
6	152	15.2	27	68.6	48	121.9
7	178	17.8	28	71.1	49	124.5
8	203	20.3	29	73.7	50	127.0

mm=millimetres

cm=centimetres

RATIO

1 Average Anciennan foot = 4 Average Whimble feet

yards to metres

yards	metres	yards	metres	yards	metres	yards	metres	yards	metres
1/8	0.11	2 1/8	1.94	4 1/8	3.77	6 1/8	5.60	8 1/8	7.43
1/4	0.23	2 1/4	2.06	4 1/4	3.89	6 1/4	5.72	8 1/4	7.54
3/8	0.34	2 3/8	2.17	4 3/8	4.00	6 3/8	5.83	8 3/8	7.66
1/2	0.46	2 1/2	2.29	4 1/2	4.11	6 1/2	5.94	8 1/2	7.77
5/8	0.57	2 5/8	2.40	4 5/8	4.23	6 5/8	6.06	8 5/8	7.89
3/4	0.69	2 3/4	2.51	4 3/4	4.34	6 3/4	6.17	8 3/4	8.00
7/8	0.80	2 7/8	2.63	4 7/8	4.46	6 7/8	6.29	8 7/8	8.12
1	0.91	3	2.74	5	4.57	7	6.40	9	8.23
1 1/8	1.03	3 1/8	2.86	5 1/8	4.69	7 1/8	6.52	9 1/8	8.34
1 1/4	1.14	3 1/4	2.97	5 1/4	4.80	7 1/4	6.63	9 1/4	8.46
1 3/8	1.26	3 3/8	3.09	5 3/8	4.91	7 3/8	6.74	9 3/8	8.57
1 1/2	1.37	3 1/2	3.20	5 1/2	5.03	7 1/2	6.86	9 1/2	8.69
1 5/8	1.49	3 5/8	3.31	5 5/8	5.14	7 5/8	6.97	9 5/8	8.80
1 3/4	1.60	3 3/4	3.43	5 3/4	5.26	7 3/4	7.09	9 3/4	8.92
1 7/8	1.71	3 7/8	3.54	5 7/8	5.37	7 7/8	7.20	9 7/8	9.03
2	1.83	4	3.66	6	5.49	8	7.32	10	9.14

Index

ORDER PROJECT PACKETS AND ADDITIONAL BOOKS

For answering any questions, obtaining signed copies of this book, or ordering Project Packets, kindly call Whimble Designs at our toll-free number 877·944·6253 or visit our website at www.thewhimbles.com.

P.S. We ask that if you call "The Enchanted Place," avoid speaking with Annabelle, the Sweet Pea Whimble, as she can be forgetful and your request could easily get lost.